AR #
123921

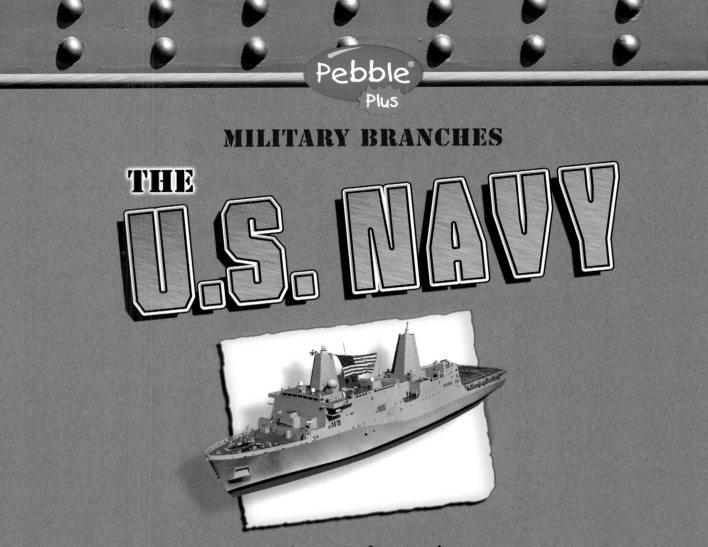

Pebble® Plus

MILITARY BRANCHES

THE U.S. NAVY

by Jennifer Reed

Consulting Editor: Gail Saunders-Smith, PhD

Capstone press®

Mankato, Minnesota

Pebble Plus is published by Capstone Press,
151 Good Counsel Drive, P.O. Box 669, Mankato, Minnesota 56002.
www.capstonepress.com

1 2 3 4 5 6 13 12 11 10 09 08

Library of Congress Cataloging-in-Publication Data
Reed, Jennifer, 1967 –
    The U.S. Navy / by Jennifer Reed.
    p. cm. — (Pebble Plus. Military branches)
    Includes bibliographical references and index.
    ISBN-13: 978-1-4296-1736-9 (hardcover)
    ISBN-10: 1-4296-1736-5 (hardcover)
    1. United States. Navy — Juvenile literature. I. Title. II. Series.
VA58.4.R44 2009
359.00973 — dc22   2008001754

Summary: Simple text and photographs describe the U.S. Navy's purpose, jobs, and ships.

Editorial Credits
Gillia Olson, editor; Renée T. Doyle, designer; Jo Miller, photo researcher

Photo Credits
Capstone Press/Karon Dubke, 3
DVIC/General Dynamics Electric Boat, 19
Photo courtesy of Northrop Grumman Ship Systems, 1
Shutterstock/Derek Gordon, 11
U.S. Navy Photo by MC1 James E. Foehl, back cover, 22; by MC1 William R. Goodwin, 21; by MC2 Lolita Lewis,
    front cover; by MC2 Ron Reeves, 15; by MC3 Jason A. Johnston, 9; by MCSN Aaron Holt, 7; by PH2 Eric S.
    Logsdon, 13; by PH3 Douglas G. Morrison, 17; by PHAN Eben Boothby, 5

Artistic Effects
iStockphoto/Piotr Przeszlo, metal treatment, cover, 1
iStockphoto/walrusmail, rivets on metal, front and back cover, 1, 24

Capstone Press thanks Dr. Sarandis Papadopoulos, Naval Historian, for his assistance with this book.

Note to Parents and Teachers

The Military Branches set supports national science standards related to science,
technology, and society. This book describes and illustrates the U.S. Navy. The images
support early readers in understanding the text. The repetition of words and phrases
helps early readers learn new words. This book also introduces early readers to
subject-specific vocabulary words, which are defined in the Glossary section. Early
readers may need assistance to read some words and to use the Table of Contents,
Glossary, Read More, Internet Sites, and Index sections of the book.

Table of Contents

What Is the Navy?

The Navy is a branch of the
United States Armed Forces.
The Navy guards the sea
to keep the country safe.

Navy Jobs

All people in the Navy
are called sailors.

Some sailors are navigators.

They plan which way
Navy ships will travel.

Some sailors are mechanics.

They fix machines.

Navy pilots fly airplanes.

Air controllers tell pilots

when to take off and land.

The Navy has special forces.
Navy SEALs are trained
to fight on land and sea.
Underwater, Navy divers fix
ships and search the ocean.

U.S. Navy SEALs

Navy Ships

Aircraft carriers are
the largest Navy ships.
They are floating airports.

Destroyers and cruisers
are warships.
They shoot large guns
and missiles.

Submarines travel underwater.

They fire underwater missiles

called torpedoes.

Keeping Us Safe

The brave sailors

of the Navy

protect our country.

Their teamwork keeps us safe.

Glossary

Armed Forces — the whole military; the U.S. Armed Forces include the Army, Navy, Air Force, Marine Corps, and Coast Guard.

branch — a part of a larger group

guard — to watch over

missile — a weapon that is fired at a target to blow it up

sailor — a person in the Navy

SEALs — a special forces group in the Navy; SEALs stands for SEa, Air, and Land.

special forces — groups trained for very difficult and dangerous jobs in the Navy

torpedo — an underwater missile used to blow up a target

warship — a Navy ship used mainly to fight enemies

Read More

Ellis, Catherine. *Ships.* Mega Military Machines. New York: PowerKids Press, 2007.

Reed, Jennifer. *Submarines.* Mighty Machines. Mankato, Minn.: Capstone Press, 2007.

Zuehlke, Jeffrey. *Warships.* Pull-Ahead Books. Minneapolis: Lerner, 2006.

Internet Sites

FactHound offers a safe, fun way to find Internet sites related to this book. All of the sites on FactHound have been researched by our staff.

Here's how:

1. Visit *www.facthound.com*

2. Choose your grade level.

3. Type in this book ID **1429617365** for age-appropriate sites. You may also browse subjects by clicking on letters, or by clicking on pictures and words.

4. Click on the **Fetch It** button.

FactHound will fetch the best sites for you!

Index

Word Count: 131
Grade: 1
Early-Intervention Level: 22